Perl 5
Pocket Reference

Third Edition

Johan Vromans

O'REILLY®

Beijing • Cambridge • Farnham • Köln • Paris • Sebastopol • Taipei • Tokyo

Perl 5 Pocket Reference, Third Edition

by Johan Vromans

Published by O'Reilly & Associates, Inc., 101 Morris Street,
Sebastopol, CA 95472.

Editor: Linda Mui

Production Editor: Johan Vromans

Production Coordinator: Colleen Gorman

Printing History:

February 1996:	First Edition.
August 1998:	Second Edition.
May 2000:	Third Edition.

0-596-00032-4
[C]

[1/01]

Table of Contents

Foreword

It's really hard to write a foreword about something that is perfect.

Now if I were writing about Perl, I could write all day, because Perl is far from perfect. But I really want to write about this pocket reference, and Johan has made it extremely difficult. I feel like Goldilocks in the wrong house–there's no story to tell when all the porridge is the right temperature, all the chairs fit perfectly, and all the beds are waterbeds. Maybe it'll get interesting later when the bears come home. No, wait, she's at the wrong house, so that won't happen either.

Ah, well. I guess this will just have to be one of boring forewords that say obvious things like: I think Johan is a great guy and has done a wonderful job in producing this perfect little booklet.

Agghh! There we are back to perfect again. I can't stand it. Just a second, there *has* to be something wrong in here somewhere. Hang on . . .

Let's see. Hmm. Table of Contents. Fits perfectly onto two pages. All section titles meaningful. Hmm, nothing wrong there.

Command line, great place to start, all the options perfectly formatted. Nope, nothing there. Basic syntax nicely summarized. (Gotta love those little information markers.) Data types, interpolation, operators . . . all good stuff. Darn. There has to be something out of whack . . .

Aha! Found it! The operator precedence table doesn't fit on one page–it's too big. (No, wait, that's my fault. Never mind.)

Control flow is under control, modules well packaged, pragmas presented pragmatically, nothing objectionable in objects. Hmm. Functions are functionally categorized, with just the right amount of description. Regular expressions are well regulated. File ops are neatly filed. I/O is handled, formats formatted, and tying neatly tied up. System interaction is systematized. Plus a bunch of miscellaneous stuff at the end, right where it belongs. How can I say anything interesting about all this? Maybe the index?

Nope, the index is perfect, too. Sigh. As our favorite little blond would say, "Everything is juuuuust right!"

Looks like Goldilocks might be staying in this house for a long, long time. Who knows, maybe she'll even live happily ever after. This just hasn't been my day. The way things have been going, Goldilocks's new house will have three computers in it, and right there beside each one will be a copy of this booklet. Argh!

Really, I can only think of one thing wrong with this pocket reference: it came too late. It would have made things ever so much easier if I'd had it *before* I started writing Perl . . .

Larry Wall
April 2000

Perl 5 Pocket Reference

Introduction

The *Perl 5 Pocket Reference* is a quick reference guide to Larry Wall's Perl programming language. It contains a concise description of all statements, functions, and variables, and lots of other useful information. This edition is based on Perl version 5.6.

The purpose of the Pocket Reference is to aid users of Perl in finding the syntax of specific functions and statements, and the meaning of built-in variables. It is *not* a self-contained user guide; basic knowledge of the Perl language is required. It is also *not* complete; some of the more obscure variants of Perl constructs have been left out. But all functions and variables are mentioned in at least one way they can be used.

See Appendix B, "Perl Links" on page 85 for more information on Perl resources.

Conventions

this	denotes text that you enter literally.
this	means variable text, i.e., things you must fill in.
this†	means that if *this* is omitted, $_ will be used instead.
word	is a keyword, i.e., a word with a special meaning.
[. . .]	denotes an optional part.
🔁	points to related documentation, usually a perldoc command.

Command-Line Options

--   Stops processing options.

-0 [*octnum*]

    (That's the number zero.) Designates an initial octal value for the record separator $/. See also -1 below.

-a   Turns on autosplit mode when used with -n or -p. Splits to @F.

-c   Checks syntax but does not execute. It does run **BEGIN** and **CHECK** blocks.

-C   Uses native wide-character system APIs, if supported by the system.

-d [: *module*]

    Runs the script under the indicated module. Default module is the Perl debugger. Use -de 0 to start the debugger without a script.

-D *flags*   Sets debugging flags.

-e *commandline*

    May be used to enter a single line of script. Multiple -e commands may be given to build up a multiline script.

-F *pat*   Specifies a pattern to split on if -a is in effect.

-h   Prints the Perl usage summary. Does not execute.

-i [*ext*]

    Files processed by <> are to be edited in place.

-I *dir*   The directory is prepended to the search path for Perl modules, @INC. Combined with -P, -I also tells the C preprocessor where to look for include files.

-l [*octnum*]

    (That's the letter ell.) Enables automatic line ending processing, e.g., -l013.

-m [-] *module*

    Does a **use** *module* before executing the script. *module* may be followed by an equals sign and a comma-separated list of items. With - does a **no** *module* instead.

−M [−] *module*

    Same as −m, but with more trickery.

−n   Assumes an input loop around the script. Lines are not printed.

−p   Assumes an input loop around the script. Lines are printed.

−P   Runs the C preprocessor on the script before compilation by Perl.

−s   Interprets −*xxx* on the command line as a switch and sets the corresponding variable $*xxx* in the script to 1. If the switch is of the form −*xxx*=*yyy*, the $*xxx* variable is set to *yyy*.

−S   Uses the PATH environment variable to search for the script.

−T   Turns on *taint* checking.

−u   Dumps core after compiling the script. To be used with the *undump* program (where available).

−U   Allows Perl to perform certain unsafe operations.

−v   Prints the version and patch level of your Perl executable. Does not execute anything.

−V [:*var*]

    Prints Perl configuration information, e.g., −V:man.dir. Does not execute anything.

−w   Prints warnings about possible spelling errors and other error-prone constructs in the script. Can be enabled and disabled under program control.

−W   Enables warnings permanently.

−x [*dir*]

    Extracts the program script from the input stream. If *dir* is specified, Perl switches to this directory before running the script.

−X   Disables warnings permanently.

Command-line options −D, −I, −M, −T, −U, −d, −m, and −w may also be specified using environment variable PERL5OPT. All

---

options except −M and −m may be used on the #! line of the Perl script.

📘 perldoc perlrun

Syntax

Perl is a free-format programming language. This means that in general it does not matter how a Perl program is written with regard to indentation and lines.

An exception to this rule is when the Perl compiler encounters a sharp or pound symbol (#) in the input: it then discards this symbol and everything following it up to the end of the current input line. This can be used to put comments in Perl programs. Real programmers put lots of useful comments in their programs.

There are places where whitespace does matter: within literal text, patterns, and formats.

If the Perl compiler encounters the special token __END__, it discards this symbol and stops reading input. Anything following this token is ignored by the Perl compiler, but can be read by the program when it is run, using the filehandle DATA.

When Perl is expecting a new statement and encounters a line that starts with =, it skips all input up to and including a line that starts with =cut. This is used to embed program documentation.

📘 perldoc perlsyn

Embedded Documentation

Tools exist to extract embedded documentation and generate input suitable for several formatters like troff, LaTeX, and HTML. The following commands can be used to control embedded documentation:

=back   See =over on the facing page.

`=begin` *fmt*

> Subsequent text up to a matching `=end` is only included when processed for formatter *fmt*.

`=cut`   Ends a document section.

`=end` *fmt*

> See `=begin`.

`=for` *fmt*

> The next paragraph is only included when processed for formatter *fmt*.

`=head1` *heading*

> Produces a first-level heading.

`=head2` *heading*

> Produces a second-level heading.

`=item` *text*

> See `=over` below.

`=over` *N*

> Starts an enumeration with indent *N*. Items are specified using `=item`. The enumeration is ended with `=back`.

`=pod`   Introduces a document section. Any of the = commands can be used to introduce a document section.

Each of the preceding commands applies to the paragraph of text that follows them; paragraphs are terminated by at least one empty line.

An indented paragraph is considered to be verbatim text and will be rendered as such.

Within normal paragraphs, markup sequences can be inserted:

B<*text*>   Make text bold (for switches and programs).

C<*code*>   Literal code.

E<*escape*>

> A named character, e.g., `E<lt>` means a < and `E<gt>` means a >.

F<*file*>   Filename.

I<*text*>   Italicize text (for emphasis and variables).

L<[*text* |] *ref*>

A cross reference. *text*, if present, is used for output.

S<*text*>   Do not break on spaces in this text.

X<*index*>

An index entry.

Z<>   A zero-width character.

Markup sequences may be nested. If a markup sequence has to contain > characters, use C<< ... >> or C<<< ... >>> etc. The last of the opening < *must* be followed by whitespace, and whitespace *must* precede the first of the closing >.

🔖 perldoc perlpod

Data Types

Array   Indexable list of scalar values.

Code   A piece of Perl code, e.g., a subroutine.

Filehandle

Used in input and output operations.

Format   A format to produce reports with.

Glob   All data types.

Hash   Associative array of scalar values.

Scalar   Strings, numbers, typeglobs and references.

Perl variables can have a distinct value for each of these data types simultaneously.

🔖 perldoc perldata

Quotes and Interpolation

Perl uses customary quotes to construct strings and such, but also implements a generic quoting mechanism. In the table below, q// means that anything placed between the slashes is treated as if it were placed between single quotes, but also that you may use any non-alphanumeric, non-space character instead of the slashes. Grouping characters like ( ), { }, [ ] and < > must be used in pairs.

When the quoting mechanism involves three delimiters you can also use two pairs of grouping characters, e.g., s{...}[...].

Customary	Generic	Meaning	Inter.	Page
' '	q//	Literal string	No	9
" "	qq//	Literal string	Yes	9
` `	qx//	Command execution	Yes	9
( )	qw//	Word list	No	9
//	m//	Pattern match	Yes	36
s///	s///	Pattern substitution	Yes	37
y///	tr///	Character translation	No	37
" "	qr//	Regular expression	Yes	9

The 'Inter.' column of the table above indicates whether string escape sequences are interpolated. If single quotes are used as delimiters for pattern matching or substitution, no interpolation takes place.

String escape sequences:

Sequence	Meaning
\a	ASCII Alarm (bell).
\b	ASCII Backspace.
\e	ASCII Escape.
\f	ASCII Formfeed.
\n	ASCII Newline.
\r	ASCII Return.
\t	ASCII Tab.
\053	Octal, ASCII +.
\cC	Control, Control-C.
\N{BLACK SPADE SUIT}	A named character, ♠.
\xeb	Hex, Latin-1 ë.
\x{03a3}	Unicode hex, greek Σ.

↪

Sequence	Meaning
\E	Ends \L, \Q, and \U.
\l	Lowcases the following character.
\L	Lowcases up to a \E.
\u	Titlecases the following character.
\U	Upcases until a \E is encountered.
\Q	Quotes non-word characters until a \E is encountered.

Octal escapes take up to three octal digits, including leading zeroes. The resulting value must not exceed 377 octal.

In patterns, which are like qq// strings, leading zeroes are mandatory in octal escapes to avoid interpretation as a back-reference unless the value exceeds the number of captures, or 9, whichever is lowest. Note that if it's a back-reference, the value is interpreted as decimal, not as octal.

Hex escapes take one or two hex digits.

\N requires the charnames pragma; see page 21.

Ž perldoc perlop
   perldoc perlunicode

Literal Values

Scalar Values

Array reference
        [1,2,3]
Code reference
        sub { *statements* }
Hash reference
        {key1 => val1, key2 => val2,...}
        Equivalent to: {key1, val1, key2, val2,...}.
Numeric
        123 1_234 123.4 5E-10 0xff (hex) 0377 (octal)
        0b010101 (binary)
        __LINE__ (line number in the current program).

Regular Expression

    `qr`/*string*/*modifiers*

    See the section "Regular Expressions" on page 32.

String

    `'abc'`

        Literal string, no variable interpolation or escape characters, except `\'` and `\\`.

    `"abc"`

        Variables are interpolated and escape sequences are processed.

    `` `command` ``

        Evaluates to the output of the command.

    `Class::`

        Mostly equivalent to `"Class"`.

    `1.2.3`   `v5.6.0.1`

        A string ('v-string') composed of the specified ordinals. The ordinal values may be in the Unicode range. `1.2.3` is equivalent to `"\x{1}\x{2}\x{3}"`. Suitable to be compared to other v-strings using string compare operators.

    `<<`*identifier*

        Shell-style "here document."

    `__FILE__`

        The name of the program file.

    `__PACKAGE__`

        The name of the current package.

List Values

`( ... )`   `(1,2,3)` is a list of three elements.

        `(1,2,3)[0]` is the first element from this list.

        `( )` is an empty list.

        `(1..4)` is the same as `(1,2,3,4)`, likewise `('a'..'z')`.

        `('a'..'z')[4,7,9]` is a slice of a list literal.

qw   `qw/fo br.../` is the same as `('fo','br',...)`.

`<...>`   *<pattern>* evaluates to all filenames according to the C-Shell wildcard pattern. Use `<${`*var*`}>` or `glob` $*var* (page 52) to glob from a variable.

Hash Values

`(...)`   `(key1 => val1, key2 => val2,...)`
        Equivalent to: `(key1, val1, key2, val2,...)`.

Filehandles

Pre-defined filehandles
        `STDIN, STDOUT, STDERR, ARGV, DATA`.
User-specified filehandles
        handle, $*var*.

Variables

`$var`   A simple scalar variable.

`$p = \$var`
        Now `$p` is a reference to scalar `$var`.

`$$p`   The scalar referenced by `$p`.

`@var`   An array. In scalar context, the number of elements in the array.

`$var[6]`
        7th element of array `@var`.

`$var[-1]`
        Last element of array `@var`.

`$p = \@var`
        Now `$p` is a reference to array `@var`.

`$$p[6]`   7th element of array referenced by `$p`.
        Also: `$p->[6]`.

`$p = \$var[6]`
        Now `$p` is a reference to the 7th element of array `@var`.

`$p = [1,3,'ape']`
> Now $p is a reference to an anonymous array with three elements.

`$var[$i][$j]`
> $j-th element of $i-th element of array @var .

`$#var`   Last index of array @var .

`@var[3,4,5]`
> A slice of array @var .

`%var`   A hash. In scalar context, true if the hash has elements.

`$var{'red'}`
> A value from hash %var .

`$p = \%var`
> Now $p is a reference to hash %var .

`$$p{'red'}`
> A value from the hash referenced by $p .
> Also: $p->{'red'} .

`$p = {red => 1, blue => 2, yellow => 3}`
> Now $p is a reference to an anonymous hash with three elements.

`@var{'a','b'}`
> A slice of %var; same as ($var{'a'},$var{'b'}) .

`$var{'a',1,...}`
> Multi-dimensional hash (obsolete).

`$c = \&mysub`
> Now $c is a reference to subroutine mysub .

`&$c( args )`
> Calls the subroutine via the reference.
> Also $c->(args) .

`$c = sub {...}`
> Now $c is a reference to an anonymous subroutine.

pkg::*var*
> A variable from a package, e.g., $pkg::var, @pkg::ary .

---

name   Symbol table entry (typeglob).
          `*n1{SCALAR}` is the same as `\$n1`, `*n1{ARRAY}`
          is the same as `\@n1`. Other possibilities are `HASH`,
          `CODE`, `GLOB` and `IO`.
          `*n1 = *n2` makes all n1 aliases for n2 .
          `*n1 = \$n2` makes the package variable $n1 an alias
          for $n2 .

You can always use a *block* (see page 14) returning the
right type of reference instead of the variable identifier, e.g.,
`${ ... }`, `&{ ... }` . `$$p` is just a shorthand for `${$p}` .

📖 `perldoc perldata`
   `perldoc perlref`

Context

Perl expressions are always evaluated in a context that
determines the outcome of the evaluation.

Boolean
          A special form of scalar context in which it only
          matters if the result is true or false.
          Anything that is undefined or evaluates to an
          empty string, the number zero, or the string "0" is
          considered false, everything else is true (including
          strings like "00").

List   A list value is expected. Arrays, hashes and slices of
          arrays, hashes and lists are also acceptable.

Scalar   A single scalar value is expected.

Void   No value is expected. If a value is provided, it is
          discarded.

The following functions relate to context:

scalar *expr*
          Forces scalar context for the expression.

wantarray
          Returns true in list context, false in scalar context,
          and **undef** in void context.

Operators and Precedence

Perl operators have the following associativity and precedence, listed from highest precedence to lowest. Table cells indicate groups of operators of equal precedence.

Assoc.	Operators	Description
right	terms and list operators	See below.
left	->	Infix dereference operator.
none	++	Auto-increment (magical on strings).
	--	Auto-decrement.
right	**	Exponentiation.
right	\	Reference to an object (unary).
right	! ~	Unary negation, bitwise complement.
right	+ -	Unary plus, minus.
left	=~	Binds a scalar expression to a pattern match.
left	!~	Same, but negates the result.
left	* / % x	Multiplication, division, modulo, repetition.
left	+ - .	Addition, subtraction, concatenation.
left	>> <<	Bitwise shift right, bitwise shift left.
right	named unary operators	E.g. sin, chdir, -f, -M.
none	< > <= >=	Numerical relational operators.
	lt gt le ge	String relational operators.
none	== != <=>	Numerical equal, not equal, compare.
	eq ne cmp	Stringwise equal, not equal, compare.
		Compare operators return −1 (less), 0 (equal), or 1 (greater).
left	&	Bitwise AND.
left	| ^	Bitwise OR, exclusive OR.
left	&&	Logical AND.
left	||	Logical OR.
none	..	Range operator.
	...	Alternative range operator.

↪

Assoc.	Operators	Description
right	? :	*if* ? *then* : *else* operator.
right	= += -= etc.	Assignment operators.
left	,	Comma operator, also list element separator.
left	=>	Same, enforces the left operand to be a string.
right	list operators (rightward)	See below.
right	not	Low precedence logical NOT.
left	and	Low precedence logical AND.
left	or	Low precedence logical OR.
left	xor	Low precedence logical XOR.

Parentheses can be used to group an expression into a term.

A list consists of expressions, variables, arrays, hashes, slices, or lists, separated by commas. It will always be interpreted as one flat series of values.

Perl functions that can be used as list operators have either very high or very low precedence, depending on whether you look at the left side of the operator or at the right side of the operator. Parentheses can be added around the parameter lists to avoid precedence problems.

The logical operators do not evaluate the right operand if the result is already known after evaluation of the left operand.

🛈 perldoc perlop

perldoc perlfunc

perldoc -f *func* will provide extensive info on the named function.

Statements

A statement is an expression, optionally followed by a modifier, and terminated with a semicolon. Statements can be combined to form a *block* when enclosed in {}. The semicolon may be omitted after the last statement of a block.

Execution of expressions can depend on other expressions using one of the modifiers if, unless, for, foreach, while, or until, e.g.:

> *expr1* if *expr2* ;
> *expr1* foreach *list* ;
> *expr1* until *expr2* ;

The logical operators | |, &&, or ? : also allow conditional execution:

> *expr1* | | *expr2* ;
> *expr1* && *expr2* ;
> *expr1* ? *expr2* : *expr3* ;

Blocks may be used for conditional execution:

> if (*expr*) *block* [[elsif (*expr*) *block* ...] else *block*]
> unless (*expr*) *block* [else *block*]

Loop blocks:

> [*label*:] while (*expr*) *block* [continue *block*]
> [*label*:] until (*expr*) *block* [continue *block*]
> [*label*:] for ([*expr*] ; [*expr*] ; [*expr*]) *block*
> [*label*:] foreach *var*†(*list*) *block* [continue *block*]
> [*label*:] *block* [continue *block*]

In foreach, the iteration variable (default: $_) is aliased to each element of the list, so modifying this variable modifies the actual list element.

The keywords for and foreach can be used interchangeably.

In loop blocks, program flow can be controlled with:

goto *label*

> Finds the statement labeled with *label* and resumes execution there. *label* may be an expression that evaluates to the name of a label.

last [*label*]

> Immediately exits the loop in question. Skips the continue block.

---

next [*label*]

> Executes the **continue** block and starts the next iteration of the loop.

redo [*label*]

> Restarts the loop block without evaluating the conditional again. Skips the **continue** block.

Special forms are:

> **do** *block* **while** *expr* ;
> **do** *block* **until** *expr* ;

which are guaranteed to perform *block* once before testing *expr*, and

> **do** *block*

which effectively turns *block* into an expression.

Subroutines

Subroutines need to be *declared*, i.e., specified how they should be called, and *defined*, i.e., specified what they should do when called.

sub *name* [(*proto*)] [*attributes*]

> Declares *name* as a subroutine, optionally specifying the prototype and attributes. Declaring a subroutine is optional, but allows the subroutine to be called just like Perl's built-in operators.

sub [*name*] [(*proto*)] [*attributes*] *block*

> Defines subroutine *name*, with optional prototype and attributes. If the subroutine has been declared with a prototype or attributes, the definition should have the same prototype and attributes.
> When *name* is omitted, the subroutine is anonymous and the definition returns a reference to the code.

When a subroutine is called, the statements in *block* are executed. Parameters are passed as a flat list of scalars as array @_. The elements of @_ are aliases for the scalar parameters.

The call returns the value of the last expression evaluated. wantarray (page 12) can be used to determine the context in which the subroutine was called.

Subroutines that have an empty prototype and do nothing but return a fixed value are inlined, e.g., sub PI() { 3.1415 }.

attributes are introduced with a : (colon). The following attributes are currently implemented:

method   The subroutine is a method.
locked   The subroutine must be locked against
            concurrent access.
lvalue   The subroutine returns a variable that can be
            assigned to.

See also pragma attributes on page 20.

There are several ways to call a subroutine.

name ([*parameters*])
            The most common way. The parameters are passed
            by reference as array @_.

&*name* ([*parameters*])
            Prototype specifications, if any, are ignored.

&*name*   The current @_ is passed directly to the called
            subroutine.

name [*arguments*]
            If the subroutine has been declared, or defined,
            it may be called as a built-in operator, without
            parentheses.

In all cases, *name* can be an expression yielding a reference to a code object. If so, you can also use &${*expr*}([*arguments*]) or ${*expr*}->([*arguments*]).

caller [*expr*]
            Returns a list ($package, $file, $line, ...) for
            a specific subroutine call. caller returns this
            information for the current subroutine, caller(1)
            for the caller of this subroutine etc. Returns false if
            no caller.

---

defined &*subname*

> Tests whether the named subroutine has been defined (has a body).

do *subroutine list*

> Deprecated form of &*subroutine*.

exists &*subname*

> Tests whether the named subroutine has been declared, either in full (with a body) or with a forward declaration.

goto &*subname*

> Substitutes a call to *subname* for the current subroutine.

prototype *name*

> Returns the prototype for the named function as a string, or **undef** if the function has no usable prototype.

return [*expr*]

> Returns from a subroutine, **eval** or **do** *file* with the value specified; if no value, returns **undef** in scalar context and an empty list in list context.

[sub] **BEGIN** *block*
[sub] **CHECK** *block*
[sub] **INIT** *block*
[sub] **END** *block*

> Normally, a Perl program is compiled and, when the compilation is successful, it is executed by the Perl interpreter.

> During compilation, **BEGIN** blocks are executed immediately when compilation of the block is complete. This happens even when only checking syntax (the −c command line option was passed to Perl). **CHECK**, **INIT**, and **END** blocks are saved.

> When the compilation finishes, any saved **CHECK** blocks are executed in reverse order. This happens even when just checking syntax, or when the program contains syntax errors.

If the compilation is successful, and the -c command line option was not passed, any saved **INIT** blocks are executed, and the Perl interpreter starts executing the program.

When the program finishes, any saved **END** blocks are executed in reverse order, and the Perl interpreter terminates. Inside the **END** blocks, $? contains the status the program is going to **exit** with.

Ⱬ `perldoc perlsub`

Packages and Modules

import *module* [*list*]

Usually imports subroutines and variables from *module* into the current package. **import** is not a built-in, but an ordinary class method that may be inherited from UNIVERSAL.

no *module* [*list*]

At compile time, **requires** the module and calls its **unimport** method on *list*. See **use** on the next page.

package [*namespace*]

Designates the remainder of the current block or file as a package with a namespace, or without one if *namespace* is omitted.

require *version*

Requires Perl to be at least this version. *version* can be numeric like 5.005, or a v-string like v5.6.0 or 5.6.1.

require *expr†*

If *expr* is numeric, behaves like **require** *version*. Otherwise *expr* must be the name of a file that is included from the Perl library. Does not include more than once, and yields a fatal error if the file does not evaluate to true. If *expr* is a bare word, assumes extension .pm for the name of the file.

---

unimport *module* [*list*]

> Usually cancels the effects of a previous **import** or **use**. Like **import**, **unimport** is not a built-in, but an ordinary class method.

use *version*

> Requires Perl to be at least this version. *version* can be numeric like 5.005, or a v-string like v5.6.0 or 5.6.1.

use *module* [*version*] [*list*]

> At compile time, **requires** the module, optionally verifies the version, and calls its **import** method on *list*. Normally used to import a list of variables and subroutines from the named module into the current package.

ℹ perldoc perlmod

Pragmatic Modules

Pragmatic modules affect the compilation of your program. Pragmatic modules can be activated (imported) with **use** and deactivated with **no**. These are usually lexically scoped.

attributes

> Provides two subroutines, attributes::get to get the attributes of a reference, and attributes::reftype that returns the Perl base type of a reference.

autouse *module* => *funcs*

> The module will not be loaded until one of the named functions is called.

base *classes*

> Establishes an IS-A relationship with the named classes at compile time.

blib [*dir*]

> Uses the MakeMaker's uninstalled version of a package. *dir* defaults to the current directory. Used for testing of uninstalled packages.

`bytes`   Treat character data as strict 8-bit bytes, as opposed to Unicode UTF-8.

`charnames` [*sets*]
    Enables character names to be expanded in strings using \N escapes.

`constant` *name* => *value*
    Defines *name* to represent a constant value.

`diagnostics` [*verbosity*]
    Forces verbose warning diagnostics and suppression of duplicate warnings.
    `use diagnostics "-verbose"` makes it even more verbose.

`fields` *names*
    Implements compile-time class fields using pseudo-hashes.

`filetest` [*strategy*]
    Changes the way the file test operators (page 38) get their information. Standard strategy is `"stat"`, alternative is `"access"`.

`integer`   Enables integer arithmetic instead of double precision floating point.

`less` *what*
    Requests less of something from the compiler (unimplemented).

`lib` *names*
    Adds libraries to `@INC`, or removes them, at compile time.

`locale`   Uses POSIX locales for built-in operations.

`open`   Establish I/O disciplines (not yet implemented).

`ops` *operations*
    Restricts unsafe operations when compiling.

`overload` *operator* => *subref*
    Overloads Perl operators. *operator* is the operator (as a string), *subref* a reference to the subroutine handling the overloaded operator.

---

re *behaviors*

> Alters regular expression behavior.
>
> use re "eval" allows patterns to contain assertions that execute Perl code, even when the pattern contains interpolated variables (see page 33).
>
> use re "taint" propagates tainting.
>
> use re "debug" and use re "debugcolor" produce debugging info.

sigtrap *info*

> Enables simple signal handling. *info* is a list of signals, e.g., qw(SEGV TRAP).

strict [*constructs*]

> Restricts unsafe constructs.
>
> use strict "refs" restricts the use of symbolic references.
>
> use strict "vars" requires all variables to be either predefined by Perl, imported, global or lexical scoped, or fully qualified.
>
> use strict "subs" restricts the use of bareword identifiers that are not subroutines.
>
> Without *constructs*, affects all of them.

subs *names*

> Predeclares subroutine names, allowing you to use them without parentheses even before they are declared.
>
> Example: use subs qw(ding dong);

vars *names*

> Predeclares variable names, allowing you to use them without being fully qualified under the strict pragma.
>
> Obsolete, use our (page 57) instead.

warnings [*class*]

> Controls built-in warnings for classes of conditions.

vmsish [*features*]

> Controls VMS-specific language features. VMS only.

use vmsish "exit" enables VMS-style exit codes.
use vmsish "status" allows system commands
to deliver VMS-style exit codes to the calling
program.
use vmsish "time" makes all times relative to the
local time zone.
Without *features*, affects all of them.

i perldoc perlmodlib

Object-Oriented Programming

An *object* is a referent that happens to know which class it
belongs to.

A *class* is a package that happens to provide methods. If a
package fails to provide a method, the base classes as listed
in @ISA are searched, depth first.

A *method* is a subroutine that expects an invocant (an object
reference or, for static methods, a package name) as the first
argument.

bless *ref* [, *classname*]
> Turns the referent referenced by *ref* into an object
> in *classname* (default is the current package).
> Returns the reference.

invocant–>method parameters
> Call the named method.

method invocant parameters
> Alternative way of calling a method, using the
> sometimes ambiguous *indirect object* syntax.

See also **ref** (page 57), attributes::reftype (page 20) and
the next section.

i perldoc perlobj
   perldoc perlboot
   perldoc perltoot

Special Classes

The special class UNIVERSAL contains methods that are automatically inherited by all other classes:

can *method*

> Returns a reference to the method if its invocant has it, **undef** otherwise.

isa *class* Returns true if its invocant is *class*, or any class inheriting from *class*.

VERSION [*need*]

> Returns the version of its invocant. Checks the version if *need* is supplied.

The pseudopackage CORE provides access to all Perl built-in functions, even when they have been overridden.

The pseudopackage SUPER provides access to an overridden base class method without having to specify which class defined that method. This is meaningful only when used inside a method.

Arithmetic Functions

abs *expr*†

> Returns the absolute value of its operand.

atan2 *y*, *x*

> Returns the arctangent of y/x in the range $-\frac{\pi}{2}$ to $+\frac{\pi}{2}$.

cos *expr*†

> Returns the cosine of *expr* (expressed in radians).

exp *expr*†

> Returns *e* to the power of *expr*.

int *expr*† Returns the integer portion of *expr*.

log *expr*†

> Returns the natural logarithm (base *e*) of *expr*.

not *expr* Logically negates the truth value of *expr*.

rand [*expr*]

> Returns a random fractional number between 0

(inclusive) and the value of *expr* (exclusive).
If *expr* is omitted, it defaults to 1.

sin *expr*†

Returns the sine of *expr* (expressed in radians).

sqrt *expr*†

Returns the square root of *expr*.

srand [*expr*]

Sets the random number seed for the **rand** operator.
If *expr* is omitted, uses some semi-random value.

time

Returns the number of non-leap seconds since
whatever time the system considers to be the epoch.
Suitable for feeding to **gmtime** and **localtime**.

Conversion Functions

chr *expr*†

Returns the character represented by the decimal
value *expr*.

gmtime [*expr*]

In list context, converts a time as returned by the
time function to a 9-element list with the time
localized for the standard Greenwich Mean Time
(UTC, or Zulu).

In scalar context, returns a formatted string, e.g.,
`"Thu May  4 20:42:00 2000"`.

Use the standard module `Time::gmtime` for by-
name access to the elements of the list; see **localtime**
below.

hex *expr*†

Returns the decimal value of *expr* interpreted as an
hexadecimal string. The string may, but need not,
start with `0x`. For other conversions, see **oct** on the
next page.

localtime [*expr*]

Like **gmtime**, but with the time localized for the local
time zone.

Use the standard module Time::localtime for by-name access to the elements of the list:

Index	Name	Description
0	sec	Seconds.
1	min	Minutes.
2	hour	Hours.
3	mday	Day in the month.
4	mon	Month, 0 = January.
5	year	Years since 1900.
6	wday	Day in week, 0 = Sunday.
7	yday	Day in year, 0 = January 1st.
8	isdst	True during daylight savings time.

oct *expr*†

>Returns the decimal value of *expr* interpreted as an octal string. If the string starts off with 0x, it will be interpreted as a hexadecimal string; if it starts off with 0b, it will be interpreted as a binary string.

ord *expr*†

>Returns the ordinal value of the first character of *expr*.

vec *expr*, *offset*, *bits*

>Treats string *expr* as a vector of unsigned integers of *bits* bits each, and yields the decimal value of the element at *offset*. *bits* must be a power of 2 greater than 0. May be assigned to.

Structure Conversion

pack *template*, *list*

>Packs the values in *list* into a sequence of bytes, using the specified template. Returns this sequence as a string.

unpack *template*, *expr*

>Unpacks the sequence of bytes in *expr* into a list, using *template*.

---

template is a sequence of characters as follows:

a / A	Byte string, null- / space-padded
b / B	Bit string in ascending / descending order
c / C	Signed / unsigned byte value
f / d	Single / double float in native format
h / H	Hex string, low / high nybble first
i / I	Signed / unsigned integer value
l / L	Signed / unsigned long value
n / N	Short / long in network (big endian) byte order
p / P	Pointer to a null-terminated / fixed-length string
q / Q	Signed / unsigned quad value
s / S	Signed / unsigned short value
u / U	Uuencoded string / Unicode UTF-8 character code
v / V	Short / long in VAX (little endian) byte order
w	A BER encoded integer
x / X	Null byte (skip forward) / Back up a byte
Z / @	Null-terminated string / null fill to position

The size of an integer, as used by i and I, depends on the system architecture. Nybbles, bytes, shorts, longs, and quads are always exactly 4, 8, 16, 32, and 64 bits respectively. Characters s, S, l, and L may be followed by a ! to signify native shorts and longs instead.

Each character may be followed by a decimal number that will be used as a repeat count; an asterisk (*) specifies all remaining arguments.

If the format is preceded with %*n*, **unpack** returns an *n*-bit checksum instead. *n* defaults to 16.

Whitespace may be included in the template for readability, and a # character may be used to introduce comments.

A special case is a numeric character code followed by a slash and a string character code, e.g. C/a; here the numeric value determines the length of the string item.

q and Q are only available if Perl has been built with 64-bit support.

String Functions

chomp *list*†

Removes $/ (page 62) from all elements of the list; returns the (total) number of characters removed.

chop *list*†

Chops off the last character on all elements of the list; returns the last chopped character.

crypt *plaintext* , *salt*

Encrypts a string (irreversibly).

eval *expr*†

expr is parsed and executed as if it were a Perl program. The value returned is the value of the last expression evaluated. If there is a syntax error or runtime error, **undef** is returned by **eval**, and $@ is set to the error message. See also **eval** on page 56.

index *str* , *substr* [, *offset*]

Returns the position of *substr* in *str* at or after *offset*. If the substring is not found, returns −1.

lc *expr*†   Returns a lowercase version of *expr*. See also \L on page 8.

lcfirst *expr*†

Returns *expr* with its first character in lowercase. See also \l on page 8.

length *expr*†

Returns the length in characters of *expr*.

quotemeta *expr*†

Returns *expr* with all regular expression metacharacters quoted. See also \Q on page 8.

rindex *str* , *substr* [, *offset*]

Returns the position of the last *substr* in *str* at or before *offset*. If the substring is not found, returns −1.

substr *expr*, *offset* [, *len* [, *newtext*]]

Extracts a substring of length *len* starting at *offset* out of *expr* and returns it. If *offset* is negative, counts from the end of the string. If *len* is negative, leaves that many characters off the end of the string. Replaces the substring with *newtext* if specified. May be assigned to.

uc *expr*†

Returns an uppercase version of *expr*. See also \U on page 8.

ucfirst *expr*†

Returns *expr* with its first character titlecased. See also \u on page 8.

Array and Hash Functions

defined *expr*†

Not specifically an array or hash function, but a convenient way to test whether an array or hash element has a defined value.

delete *lku*
delete @*array*[*index1*, ...]
delete @*hash*{ *key1*, *key2*, ... }

lku must an array lookup like $*array*[*index*] or *expr*->[*index*], or a hash key lookup like $*hash*{ *key*} or *expr*->{ *key*}. Deletes the specified elements from the array or hash. Returns aliases to the deleted value(s). Deleting the last element(s) of an array will shorten the array.

each %*hash*

In list context, returns a 2-element list consisting of the key and an alias to the value for the next element of the hash. In scalar context, returns only the key. Entries are returned in an apparently random order. After all values of the hash have been returned, an empty list is returned. The next call to **each** after that will start iterating again. A call to **keys** or **values** will reset the iteration.

exists *lku*

lku must an array indexing or a hash key lookup

(see **delete** on the preceding page). Checks whether the specified array element or hash key exists.

grep *expr* , *list*
grep *block list*

> Evaluates *expr* or *block* for each element of the list, locally aliasing $_ to the element. In list context, returns the list of elements from *list* for which *expr* or *block* returned true. In scalar context, returns the number of such elements.

join *expr* , *list*

> Returns the string formed by inserting *expr* between all elements of *list* and concatenating the result.

keys %*hash*

> In list context, returns a list of all the keys of the named hash. In scalar context, returns the number of elements of the hash.
>
> Can be assigned to, to pre-extend the hash.

map *expr* , *list*
map *block list*

> Evaluates *expr* or *block* for each element of the list, locally aliasing $_ to the element. Returns the list of results.

pop [@*array*]

> Pops off and returns the last value of the array. If @*array* is omitted, pops @_ if inside a subroutine, else pops @ARGV.

push @*array* , *list*

> Pushes the values of the list onto the end of the array. Returns the length of the resultant array.

reverse *list*

> In list context, returns the list in reverse order. In scalar context, concatenates the list elements and returns the reverse of the resulting string.

scalar @*array*

> Returns the number of elements in the array.

scalar %*hash*

> Returns true if there are keys in the hash.

shift [@*array*]

> Shifts the first value of the array off and returns it,
> shortening the array by 1 and moving everything
> down. If @*array* is omitted, shifts @_ if inside a
> subroutine, else shifts @ARGV.

sort [*subroutine*] *list*

> Sorts the *list* and returns the sorted list value.
> *subroutine*, if specified, must return less than zero,
> zero, or greater than zero, depending on how the
> elements of the list are to be ordered.
>
> *subroutine* may be (a variable containing) the
> name of a user-defined routine, or a *block*. If the
> subroutine has been declared with a prototype of
> ($$), the values to be compared are passed as
> normal parameters; otherwise, they are available to
> the routine as package global variables $a and $b.

splice @*array*, *offset* [, *length* [, *list*]]

> Removes the elements of @*array* designated by
> *offset* and *length*, and replaces them with *list* (if
> specified). Returns the elements removed. If *offset*
> is negative, counts from the end of the array.

split [*pattern* [, *expr*† [, *limit*]]]

> Splits *expr* (a string) into a list of strings, and returns
> it. If *limit* is a positive number, splits into at most
> that number of fields. A negative value indicates all
> fields. If *limit* is omitted, or 0, trailing empty fields
> are not returned.
>
> If *pattern* is omitted, splits at the whitespace (after
> skipping any leading whitespace). If not in list
> context, returns number of fields and splits to @_.
> See also the section "Search and replace functions"
> on page 36.

unshift @*array*, *list*

> Prepends *list* to the front of the array. Returns the
> length of the resultant array.

---

values %*hash*

        Returns a list consisting of aliases to all the values of the named hash.

Regular Expressions

Each character matches itself, unless it is one of the special characters +?.*^$(){[|\. The special meaning of these characters can be escaped using a \.

The *multiline* and *single-line* modes are discussed in the section "Search and Replace Functions" on page 36.

.   Matches any character, but not a newline. In single-line mode, matches newlines as well.

(...)   Groups a series of pattern elements to a single element. The text the group matches is captured for later use.

^   Matches the beginning of the target. In multiline mode, also matches after every newline character.

$ Matches the end of the line, or before a final newline character. In multiline mode, also matches before *every* newline character.

[...]   Denotes a class of characters to match. [^ ...] negates the class.

... | ... | ...

        Matches the alternatives from left to right, until one succeeds.

(?# *text*)

        Comment.

(? [*modifier*] : *pattern*)

        Like (*pattern*) but does not capture the text it matches.

        modifier can be one or more of i, m, s, or x. Modifiers can be switched off by preceding the letter(s) with a minus sign, e.g., si-xm.

        See page 36 for the meaning of the modifiers.

(?= *pattern*)

>Zero-width positive look-ahead assertion.

(?! *pattern*)

>Zero-width negative look-ahead assertion.

(?<= *pattern*)

>Zero-width positive look-behind assertion.

(?<! *pattern*)

>Zero-width negative look-behind assertion.

(?{ *code* })

>Executes Perl code while matching. Always succeeds with zero width. Can be used as the condition in a conditional pattern selection. If not, the result of executing *code* is stored in $^R.

(??{ *code* })

>Executes Perl code while matching. Interprets the result as a pattern.

(?> *pattern*)

>Like (?: *pattern*), but prevents backtracking inside.

(?(*cond*) *ptrue* [| *pfalse*])

>Selects a pattern depending on the condition. *cond* should be the number of a parenthesized subpattern, or one of the zero-width look-ahead, look-behind and evaluate assertions.

(? *modifier*)

>Embedded pattern-match modifier. *modifier* can be one or more of i, m, s, or x. Modifiers can be switched off by preceding the letter(s) with a minus sign, e.g., (?si-xm).

Quantified subpatterns match as many times as possible. When followed with a ? they match the minimum number of times. These are the quantifiers:

+ Matches the preceding pattern element one or more times.

? Matches zero or one times.

| `*` | Matches zero or more times. |
| `{n,m}` | Denotes the minimum *n* and maximum *m* match count. `{n}` means exactly *n* times; `{n,}` means at least *n* times. |

Patterns are processed as double-quoted strings, so standard string escapes (see page 7) have their usual meaning. An exception is \b, which matches word boundaries, except when in a character class, where it denotes a backspace again.

A \ escapes any special meaning of non-alphanumeric characters, but it turns most alphanumeric characters into something special:

`\1...\9`	Refer to matched subexpressions, grouped with ( ). \10 and up can also be used if the pattern has that many subexpressions.
`\w`	Matches alphanumeric plus _, \W matches non-\w.
`\s`	Matches whitespace, \S matches non-whitespace.
`\d`	Matches numeric, \D matches non-numeric.
`\A`	Matches the beginning of the string.
`\Z`	Matches the end of the string, or before a newline at the end.
`\z`	Matches the physical end of the string.
`\b`	Matches word boundaries, \B matches non-boundaries.
`\G`	Matches where the previous search with a g modifier left off.
`\p`*p*	Matches a named property, \P*p* matches non-*p*. Use \p{*prop*} for names longer than one single character.
`\X`	Match extended Unicode "combining character sequence."
`\C`	Match a single 8-bit byte.

\1 and up, \d, \D, \p, \P, \s, \S, \w, and \W may be used inside and outside character classes.

POSIX classes are used inside character classes, like
[[:alpha:]]. These are the POSIX classes and their Unicode
property names:

[:alpha:] \p{IsAlpha}
> Matches one alphabetic character.

[:alnum:] \p{IsAlnum}
> Matches one alphanumeric character.

[:ascii:] \p{IsASCII}
> Matches one ASCII character.

[:cntrl:] \p{IsCntrl}
> Matches one control character.

[:digit:] \p{IsDigit}
> Matches one numeric character, like \d.

[:graph:] \p{IsGraph}
> Matches one alphanumeric or punctuation character.

[:lower:] \p{IsLower}
> Matches one lowercase character.

[:print:] \p{IsPrint}
> Matches one alphanumeric or punctuation character
> or space character.

[:punct:] \p{IsPunct}
> Matches one punctuation character.

[:space:] \p{IsSpace}
> Matches one whitespace character, like \s.

[:upper:] \p{IsUpper}
> Matches one uppercase character.

[:word:] \p{IsWord}
> Matches one word character, like \w.

[:xdigit:] \p{IsXDigit}
> Matches one hexadecimal digit.

The POSIX classes can be negated with a ^, e.g., [:^print:],
the named properties by using \P, e.g., \P{IsPrint}.

See also $1...$9, $+, $`, $&, $' on page 65, and @- and @+
on page 66.

With modifier x, whitespace and comments can be embedded in the patterns.

Regular expression patterns can be compiled and used as values with the **qr** quoting operator: qr/*string*/*modifiers* compiles *string* as a pattern according to the (optional) modifiers, and returns the compiled pattern as a scalar value.

🔲 perldoc perlre

Search and Replace Functions

[*expr* =~] [**m**] /*pattern*/ [g [c]][i][m][o][s][x]

Searches *expr* (default: $_) for a pattern.
For =~, its negation !~ may be used, which is true when =~ would return false, and vice versa.

After a successful match, the following special variables are set:

$&	The string that matched.
$`	The string preceding what was matched.
$'	The string following what was matched.
$1	The first parenthesized subexpression that matched, $2 the second, and so on.
$+	The last subexpression that matched.
@−	The start offsets of the match and submatches.
@+	The corresponding end offsets.

If used in list context, a list is returned consisting of the subexpressions matched by the parentheses in pattern, i.e., ($1,$2,$3, ...).

Optional modifiers:

c	(with g) prepares for continuation.
g	matches as many times as possible.
i	searches in a case-insensitive manner.
o	interpolates variables only once.
m	treats the string as multiple lines, ^ and $ will match at embedded newline characters.
s	treats the string as a single line, . will match embedded newline characters.
x	allows for whitespace and comments.

If *pattern* is empty, the most recent pattern from a previous successful m// or s/// is used.

With g, the match in scalar context can be used as an iterator. The iterator is reset upon failure, unless c is also supplied.

See page 6 for generic quoting rules and string interpolation.

?*pattern*?

This is just like the /*pattern*/ search, except that it matches only once between calls to the **reset** operator.

[$*var* =~] s/*pattern*/*newtext*/ [e][g][i][m][o][s][x]

Searches the string *var* (default $_) for a pattern, and if found, replaces that part with the replacement text.

If successful, sets the special variables as described with m// and returns the number of substitutions made. Otherwise, it returns false.

Optional modifiers:

g   replaces all occurrences of the pattern.

e   evaluates the replacement string as a Perl expression.

For the other modifiers, see m/*pattern*/ matching on the preceding page.

If *pattern* is empty, the most recent pattern from a previous successful m// or s/// is used.

See page 6 for generic quoting rules and string interpolation.

[$*var* =~] tr/*search*/*replacement*/ [c][d][s]

Transliterates all occurrences of the characters found in the search list into the corresponding character in the replacement list. It returns the number of characters replaced.

Optional modifiers:

c   complements the search list.

d   deletes all characters found in the search list

that do not have a corresponding character in the replacement list.

s   squeezes all sequences of characters that are translated into the same target character into one occurrence of this character.

See page 6 for generic quoting rules and string interpolation.

[$*var* =~] y/ *search*/ *replacement*/ *modifiers*

Identical to **tr**.

If the right hand side of the =~ or !~ is an expression rather than a search pattern, substitution, or transliteration, and its value is not the result of a **qr** operator, it is interpreted as a string and compiled into a search pattern at runtime.

pos *scalar*†

Returns the position where the last /g search in *scalar* left off. Alters the value of \G if assigned to.

study *scalar*†

Studies the scalar in anticipation of performing many pattern matches on its contents before the variable is next modified.

File Test Operators

These unary operators take one argument, either a filename or a filehandle, and test the associated file to see if something is true about it. If the argument is omitted, they test $_ (except for −t, which tests STDIN). If the special argument _ (underscore) is passed, they use the information from the preceding test or **stat** call.

See also the filetest pragma on page 21.

−r −w −x   File is readable/writable/executable by effective uid/gid.

−R −W −X   File is readable/writable/executable by real uid/gid.

−o −O   File is owned by effective/real uid.

-e -z	File exists/has zero size.
-s	File exists and has non-zero size. Returns the size.
-f -d	File is a plain file/a directory.
-l -S -p	File is a symbolic link/a socket/a named pipe (FIFO).
-b -c	File is a block/character special file.
-u -g -k	File has setuid/setgid/sticky bit set.
-t	Tests whether filehandle (STDIN by default) is opened to a tty.
-T -B	File is a text/non-text (binary) file. These tests return true on an empty file, or a file at EOF when testing a filehandle.
-M -A -C	File modification/access/inode-change time, expressed in fractional days. The value returned reflects the file age at the time the program started. See also $^T on page 64.

File Operations

Functions operating on a list of files return the number of files successfully operated upon.

chmod *list*

Changes the permissions of a list of files. The first element of the list must be the numerical mode. If this is a number, it must be an octal number, e.g., 0644.

chown *list*

Changes the owner and group of a list of files. The first two elements of the list must be the numerical user id and group id. If either is -1, that property is not changed.

link *oldfile* , *newfile*

Creates a new filename linked to the old file.

lstat *file*†

Like stat, but if the last component of the filename

---

is a symbolic link, **stat**s the link instead of the file it links to.

mkdir *dir* [, *perm*]

Creates a directory with permissions specified by *perm* and modified by the current umask. If *perm* is a number, it must be an octal number. Default value for *perm* is 0777.

See also **umask** on page 53.

readlink *expr*†

Returns the name of the file pointed to by the symbolic link designated by *expr*.

rename *oldname* , *newname*

Changes the name of a file.

rmdir *expr*†

Deletes the directory if it is empty.

stat *file*† Returns a 13-element list with file information. *file* can be a filehandle, an expression evaluating to a filename, or _ to refer to the last file test operation or **stat** call.

Returns an empty list if the **stat** fails.

Use the standard module `File::stat` for by-name access to the elements of the list:

Index	Name	Description
0	dev	Device code.
1	ino	Inode number.
2	mode	Type and access flags.
3	nlink	Number of hard links.
4	uid	User id of owner.
5	gid	Group id of owner.
6	rdev	Device type.
7	size	Size, in bytes.
8	atime	Timestamp of last access.
9	mtime	Timestamp of last modification.
10	ctime	Timestamp of last status change.
11	blksize	File system block size.
12	blocks	Size, in blocks.

symlink *oldfile* , *newfile*

> Creates a new filename symbolically linked to the old filename.

truncate *file* , *size*

> Truncates *file* to *size*. *file* may be a filename or a filehandle.

unlink *list*†

> Deletes a list of files.

utime *list*

> Changes the access and modification times. The first two elements of the list must be the numerical access and modification times.
> The inode change time will be set to the current time.

Input and Output

In input/output operations, *filehandle* may be a filehandle as opened by the **open** operator, a predefined filehandle (e.g., STDOUT), or a scalar variable that evaluates to a reference to or the name of a filehandle to be used.

<filehandle>

> In scalar context, reads a single record, usually a line, from the file opened on *filehandle*. In list context, reads the rest of the file.

`<>`

`<ARGV>` Reads from the input stream formed by the files specified in @ARGV, or standard input if no arguments were supplied.

binmode *filehandle* [, *discipline*]

> Arranges for the file opened on *filehandle* to be read or written using the specified discipline (default: ":raw").

close [*filehandle*]

> Closes the filehandle. Resets $. if it was an input

file. If *filehandle* is omitted, closes the currently
selected filehandle.

dbmclose *%hash*

Closes the file associated with the hash.
Superseded by **untie**, see page 50.

dbmopen *%hash*, *dbmname*, *mode*

Opens a dbm file and associates it with the hash.
Superseded by **tie**, see page 50.

eof *filehandle*

Returns true if the next read will return EOF (end of
file), or if the file is not open.

eof   Returns the EOF status for the last file read.

eof( )   Indicates EOF on the pseudo-file formed of the files
listed on the command line.

fcntl *filehandle*, *function*, $*var*

Calls system-dependent file control functions.

fileno *filehandle*

Returns the file descriptor for a given (open) file.

flock *filehandle*, *operation*

Calls a system-dependent locking routine on the
file. *operation* is formed by adding one or more
values or LOCK_ constants from the table on page 47.

getc [*filehandle*]

Returns the next character from the file, or an empty
string on end of file.
If *filehandle* is omitted, reads from STDIN.

ioctl *filehandle*, *function*, $*var*

Calls system-dependent I/O control functions.

open *filehandle* [, *modeandname*]

Opens a file and associates it with *filehandle*. If
filehandle is an uninitialized scalar variable, a new,
unique, filehandle is automatically created.
modeandname must contain the name of the file,
and the mode with which to open it.
If *modeandname* is not provided, a global (package)

variable with the same name as *filehandle* must provide the mode and name.

The following conventions apply for *modeandname*:

name   Input only.

<*name*   Input only.

>*name*   Output only. The file is created or truncated if necessary.

>>*name*   Open the file in append mode. The file is created if necessary.

+<*name*   This is the normal mode for read/write update access.

+>*name*   Write/read update access. The file is created or truncated first, so you can only reread what you just wrote.

+>>*name*
          Read/append access.

| *command*
          Opens a pipe to write to a command. If *command* is –, forks first.

command |
          Opens a pipe to read from a command. If *command* is –, forks first.

name may be – to designate standard input or output.

name may also be &*filedesc* or &=*filedesc*, in which case the new filehandle is connected (&) or aliased (&=) to the (previously opened) filehandle or descriptor.

Whitespace is allowed in *modeandname*, as a consequence this form of **open** cannot easily be used to open files with names that start or end with whitespace.

🛈   perldoc perlopentut

---

open *filehandle*, *mode*, *name* [, ...]

Opens a file *name* according to *mode* and associates it with *filehandle*. If *filehandle* is an uninitialized scalar variable, a new, unique, filehandle is automatically created.

The following open modes are possible:

<   Input only. This is the default when the *mode* is empty.

>   Output only. The file is created or truncated if necessary.

>>   Open the file in append mode. The file is created if necessary.

+<   Read/write update access.

+>   Write/read update access.

+>>   Read/append access.

|-   Opens a pipe to write to a command.

-| Opens a pipe to read from a command.

🛈 `perldoc perlopentut`

pipe *readhandle*, *writehandle*

Creates a pair of connected pipes. If either handle is an uninitialized scalar variable, a new, unique, filehandle is automatically created.

print [*filehandle*] *list*†

Prints the elements of *list*, converting them to strings if needed. If *filehandle* is omitted, prints to the currently selected output handle.

printf [*filehandle*] *list*†

Equivalent to **print** *filehandle* **sprintf** *list*.

read *filehandle*, $*var*, *length* [, *offset*]

Reads *length* binary bytes from the file into the variable at *offset*. Returns the number of bytes actually read, 0 on EOF, and **undef** on failure.

readline *expr*

Internal function that implements the < > operator.

readpipe scalar *expr*

Internal function that implements the **qx** operator. *expr* is executed as a system command.

seek *filehandle*, *position*, *whence*

Arbitrarily positions the file. *whence* can be one of the values or SEEK_ constants from the table on page 47.

select [*filehandle*]

Sets the current default filehandle for output operations if *filehandle* is supplied. Returns the currently selected filehandle.

select *rbits*, *wbits*, *nbits*, *timeout*

Performs a *select* syscall with the same parameters.

sprintf *format*, *list*

Returns a string resulting from formatting a (possibly empty) list of values. See the section "Formatted Printing" on page 47 for a complete list of format conversions. See the section "Formats" on page 49 for an alternative way to obtain formatted output.

sysopen *filehandle*, *path*, *mode* [, *perms*]

Performs an *open* syscall. The possible values and flag bits of *mode* and *perms* are system-dependent; they are available via the standard module Fcntl. If *filehandle* is an uninitialized scalar variable, a new, unique, filehandle is automatically created.

mode is formed by adding one or more values or O_ constants from the table on the next page.

🛈 perldoc perlopentut

sysread *filehandle*, $*var*, *length* [, *offset*]

Reads *length* bytes into $*var* at *offset*. Returns the number of bytes actually read, 0 on EOF, and **undef** on failure.

sysseek *filehandle*, *position*, *whence*

Arbitrarily positions the file for use with **sysread** and **syswrite**. *whence* can be one of the values or SEEK_ constants from the table on page 47.

---

syswrite *filehandle* , *scalar* [, *length* [, *offset*]]

> Writes *length* bytes from *scalar* at *offset*. Returns the number of bytes actually written, or **undef** if there was an error.

tell [*filehandle*]

> Returns the current file position for the file. If *filehandle* is omitted, assumes the file last read.

Common constants

Several input/output related constants can be imported from the standard module Fcntl.

Constants related to **open** and **sysopen** are imported by default. For some constants, the widely accepted values are shown, in octal.

Value	Name	Description
00000	O_RDONLY	Read-only access.
00001	O_WRONLY	Write-only access.
00002	O_RDWR	Read and write access.
00100	O_CREAT	Create the file if non-existent.
00200	O_EXCL	Fail if the file already exists.
02000	O_APPEND	Append data to the end of the file.
01000	O_TRUNC	Truncate the file.
	O_NONBLOCK	Non-blocking input/output.
	O_NDELAY	Same as O_NONBLOCK.
	O_SYNC	Synchronous input/output.
	O_EXLOCK	Lock exclusive.
	O_SHLOCK	Lock shared.
	O_DIRECTORY	File must be a directory.
	O_NOFOLLOW	Do not follow symlinks.
	O_BINARY	Use binary mode for input/output.
	O_LARGEFILE	Allow file to be larger than 4 Gb.
	O_NOCTTY	Terminal will not become the controlling tty.

Constants related to **seek** and **sysseek** must be imported explictly by specifying :seek in the import list of Fcntl.

Value	Name	Description
00	SEEK_SET	Seek position.
01	SEEK_CUR	Seek offset from current position.
02	SEEK_END	Seek offset from end of file.

Constants related to **flock** must be imported explictly by specifying :flock in the import list of Fcntl.

Value	Name	Description
001	LOCK_SH	Shared lock.
002	LOCK_EX	Exclusive lock.
004	LOCK_NB	Non-blocking lock.
010	LOCK_UN	Unlock.

Formatted Printing

printf and **sprintf** format a list of values according to a format string that may use the following conversions:

%%	A percent sign.
%b	An unsigned number (binary).
%c	The character corresponding to the ordinal value.
%d	A signed integer.
%e	A floating-point number (scientific notation).
%f	A floating-point number (fixed decimal notation).
%g	A floating-point number (%e or %f notation).
%i	A synonym for %d.
%n	The number of characters formatted so far is stored into the corresponding variable in the parameter list.
%o	An unsigned integer, in octal.
%p	A pointer (address in hexadecimal).
%s	A string.
%u	An unsigned integer (decimal).

%x	An unsigned integer (hexadecimal).
%D	An obsolete synonym for %ld.
%E	Like %e, but using an uppercase "E".
%F	An obsolete synonym for %f.
%G	Like %g, but with an uppercase "E" (if applicable).
%O	An obsolete synonym for %lo.
%U	An obsolete synonym for %lu.
%X	Like %x, but using uppercase letters.

The following flags can be put between the % and the conversion letter:

space	Prefix a positive number with a space.
+	Prefix a positive number with a plus sign.
−	Left-justify within the field.
0	Use zeroes instead of spaces to right-justify.
#	With o, b, x, or X: prefix a nonzero number with "0", "0b", "0x", or "0X".
number	Minimum field width.

. number

> For a floating-point number: the number of digits after the decimal point.
> For a string: the maximum length.
> For an integer: the minimum width.

h	Interpret integer as "short" or "unsigned short" according to the C type.
l	Interpret integer as "long" or "unsigned long" according to the C type.
ll, L, q	Interpret integer as "quad" (64-bit).
v	With d, o, b, x, or X: print string as series of ordinals.
V	Interpret integer according to Perl's type.

An asterisk (*) may be used instead of a number; the value of the next item in the list will be used.

With %*v, the next item will be used to separate the values.

See the section "Formats" on the next page for an alternative way to obtain formatted output.

Formats

formline *picture* , *list*

> Formats *list* according to *picture* and accumulates the result into $^A.

write [*filehandle*]

> Writes a formatted record to the specified file, using the format associated with that file.
>
> If *filehandle* is omitted, the currently selected one is taken.

Formats are defined as follows:

> format [*name*] =
> *formlist*
> .

formlist is a sequence of lines, each of which is either a comment line (# in the first column), a picture line, or an argument line.

A picture line contains descriptions of fields. It can also contain other text that will be output as given. Argument lines contain lists of values that are output in the format and order of the preceding picture line.

name defaults to STDOUT if omitted.

Picture fields are:

@<<<   Left-adjusted field. Repeat the < to denote the desired width.

@>>>   Right-adjusted field.

@| | | Centered field.

@#.## Numeric format with implied decimal point.

@*   Multiline field.

Use ^ instead of @ for multiline block filling.

Use ~ in a picture line to suppress unwanted empty lines.

Use ~~ in a picture line to have this format line repeated until it would yield a completely blank line. Use with ^ fields to have them repeated until exhausted.

Set $- to zero to force a page break on the next **write**.

See also $^, $~, $^A, $%, $:, $^L, $- and $= in the section "Special Variables" on page 61.

⚡ `perldoc perlform`

Tying Variables

tie *var*, *classname*, [*list*]
> Ties a variable to a class that will handle it. *list* is passed to the class constructor.

tied *var*   Returns a reference to the object underlying *var*, or **undef** if *var* is not tied to a class.

untie *var*
> Breaks the binding between the variable and the class.

A class implementing a tied scalar should define the methods TIESCALAR, DESTROY, FETCH, and STORE.

A class implementing a tied ordinary array should define the methods TIEARRAY, CLEAR, DESTROY, EXTEND, FETCHSIZE, FETCH, POP, PUSH, SHIFT, SPLICE, STORESIZE, STORE, and UNSHIFT.

A class implementing a tied hash should define the methods TIEHASH, CLEAR, DELETE, DESTROY, EXISTS, FETCH, FIRSTKEY, NEXTKEY, and STORE.

A class implementing a tied filehandle should define the methods TIEHANDLE, CLOSE, DESTROY, GETC, PRINTF, PRINT, READLINE, READ, and WRITE.

Several base classes to implement tied variables are available in the standard libraries: Tie::Array, Tie::Handle, Tie::Hash, Tie::RefHash, and Tie::Scalar.

⚡ `perldoc perltie`

Directory Reading Routines

closedir *dirhandle*

> Closes a directory opened by **opendir**.

opendir *dirhandle, dirname*

> Opens a directory on the handle specified. If *dirhandle* is an uninitialized scalar variable, a new, unique, handle is automatically created.

readdir *dirhandle*

> In scalar context, returns the next entry from the directory or **undef** if none remains. The entry is the name component within the directory, not the full name.
>
> In list context, returns a list of all remaining entries from the directory.

rewinddir *dirhandle*

> Positions the directory at the beginning.

seekdir *dirhandle, pos*

> Sets the position for **readdir** on the directory. *pos* should be a file offset as returned by **telldir**.

telldir *dirhandle*

> Returns the position in the directory.

System Interaction

alarm *expr†*

> Schedules a SIGALRM signal to be delivered after *expr* seconds. If *expr* is zero, cancels a pending timer.

chdir [*expr*]

> Changes the working directory.
>
> Uses $ENV{HOME} or $ENV{LOGNAME} if *expr* is omitted.

chroot *filename†*

> Changes the root directory for the process and any future children.

---

die [*list*]

> Prints the value of *list* to STDERR and exits with
> $! || ($? >> 8) || 255. *list* defaults to "Died".
> Inside an eval, the error message is stuffed into
> $@, and the **eval** is terminated returning **undef**; this
> makes **die** the way to raise an exception.

exec [*program*] *list*

> Executes the system command in *list*; does not
> return. *program* can be used to explictly designate
> the program to execute the command.

exit [*expr*]

> Exits immediately with the value of *expr*, which
> defaults to zero. Calls **END** routines and object
> destructors before exiting.

fork
> Does a *fork* syscall. Returns the process id of the
> child to the parent process (or **undef** on failure) and
> zero to the child process.

getlogin
> Returns the current login name as known by the
> system. If it returns false, use **getpwuid**.

getpgrp [*pid*]

> Returns the process group for process *pid*. If *pid* is
> zero, or omitted, uses the current process.

getppid
> Returns the process id of the parent process.

getpriority *which*, *who*

> Returns the current priority for a process, process
> group, or user. Use getpriority 0,0 to designate
> the current process.

glob *expr*†

> Returns a list of filenames that match the C-shell
> pattern(s) in *expr*. Use File::Glob for more
> detailed globbing control.

kill *list*
> Sends a signal to a list of processes. The first
> element of the list must be the signal to send, either
> numerically (e.g., 1), or its name as a string (e.g.,
> "HUP"). Negative signals affect process groups
> instead of processes.

---

setpgrp *pid*, *pgrp*

Sets the process group for the *pid*. If *pid* is zero, affects the current process.

setpriority *which*, *who*, *priority*

Sets the current priority for a process, process group, or a user.

sleep [*expr*]

Causes the program to sleep for *expr* seconds, or forever if *expr* is omitted. Returns the number of seconds actually slept.

syscall *list*

Calls the syscall specified in the first element of the list, passing the rest of the list as arguments to the call. Returns −1 (and sets $!) on error.

system [*program*] *list*

Like **exec**, except that a fork is performed first, and the parent process waits for the child process to complete.

During the wait, the signals SIGINT and SIGQUIT are passed to the child process.

Returns the exit status of the child process. Zero indicates success, not failure.

program can be used to explicitly designate the program to execute the command.

times   Returns a 4-element list (user, system, cuser, csystem) giving the user and system times, in seconds, for this process and the children of this process.

umask [*expr*]

Sets the umask for the process and returns the old one. If *expr* is a number, it must be an octal number. If *expr* is omitted, does not change the current umask value.

wait   Waits for a child process to terminate and returns the process id of the deceased process (−1 if none). The status is returned in $?.

---

waitpid *pid* , *flags*

> Performs the same function as the corresponding syscall. Returns 1 when process *pid* is dead, −1 if nonexistent.

warn [*list*]

> Prints the *list* on STDERR like **die**, but doesn't exit. *list* defaults to "Warning: something's wrong".

Networking

accept *newsocket* , *listeningsocket*

> Accepts a new socket. If *newsocket* is an uninitialized scalar variable, a new, unique, handle is automatically created.

bind *socket* , *name*

> Binds the name to the socket.

connect *socket* , *name*

> Connects a socket to the named peer.

getpeername *socket*

> Returns the socket address of the other end of the socket.

getsockname *socket*

> Returns the name of the socket.

getsockopt *socket* , *level* , *optname*

> Returns the socket options.

listen *socket* , *queuesize*

> Starts listening on the specified socket, allowing *queuesize* connections.

recv *socket* , $*var* , *length* , *flags*

> Receives a message of *length* bytes on the socket and puts it into scalar variable $*var*.

send *socket* , *msg* , *flags* [, *to*]

> Sends a message on the socket.

setsockopt *socket* , *level* , *optname* , *optval*

> Sets the requested socket option.

shutdown *socket*, *how*
> Shuts the socket down.

socket *socket*, *domain*, *type*, *protocol*
> Creates a socket in the domain with the given type and protocol. If *socket* is an uninitialized scalar variable, a new, unique, handle is automatically created.

socketpair *socket1*, *socket2*, *domain*, *type*, *protocol*
> Works the same as **socket**, but creates a pair of bidirectional sockets.

System V IPC

use the standard module IPC::SysV to access the message- and semaphore-specific operation names.

msgctl *id*, *cmd*, *args*
> Calls *msgctl*. If *cmd* is IPC_STAT then *args* must be a scalar variable.

msgget *key*, *flags*
> Creates a message queue for *key*. Returns the message queue identifier.

msgrcv *id*, $*var*, *size*, *type*, *flags*
> Receives a message from queue *id* into $*var*.

msgsnd *id*, *msg*, *flags*
> Sends *msg* to queue *id*.

semctl *id*, *semnum*, *cmd*, *arg*
> Calls *semctl*. If *cmd* is IPC_STAT or GETALL then *arg* must be a scalar variable.

semget *key*, *nsems*, *size*, *flags*
> Creates a set of semaphores for *key*. Returns the message semaphore identifier.

semop *key*, . . .
> Performs semaphore operations.

shmctl *id*, *cmd*, *arg*
> Calls *shmctl*. If *cmd* is IPC_STAT then *arg* must be a scalar variable.

shmget *key*, *size*, *flags*

> Creates shared memory. Returns the shared memory segment identifier.

shmread *id*, $*var*, *pos*, *size*

> Reads at most *size* bytes of the contents of shared memory segment *id* starting at offset *pos* into $*var*.

shmwrite *id*, *string*, *pos*, *size*

> Writes at most *size* bytes of *string* into the contents of shared memory segment *id* at offset *pos*.

i   `perldoc perlipc`

Miscellaneous

defined *expr*†

> Tests whether the scalar expression has an actual value.

do { *expr* ; ... }

> Executes the block and returns the value of the last expression. See also section "Statements" on page 14.

do *filename*

> Executes *filename* as a Perl script. See also **require** on page 19.

dump [*label*]

> Immediate core dump. When reincarnated, starts at *label*. Obsolete.

eval { *expr* ; ... }

> Executes the code between { and }. Traps runtime errors and returns as described with **eval**(*expr*) on page 28.

local [**our** [*class*]] *variable*

> Gives a temporary value to the named package variable, which lasts until the enclosing block, file, or **eval** exits.
> *variable* may be a scalar, array, hash, or an element (or slice) of an array or hash.

my [*class*] *variable*

> Creates a scope for the variable lexically local to the enclosing block, file, or **eval**.

our [*class*] *variable*

> Declares the variable to be a valid global within the enclosing block, file, or **eval**.

ref *expr*† Returns true if *expr* is a reference. Returns the package name if *expr* has been blessed into a package.

reset [*expr*]

> *expr* is a string of single letters. All variables in the current package beginning with one of those letters are reset to their pristine state.
>
> If *expr* is omitted, resets ?? searches so that they work again.

undef [*lvalue*]

> Undefines the *lvalue*. Always returns **undef**.

Information from System Databases

Information About Users

In list context, each of these routines returns a list of values. Use the standard module User::pwent for by-name access to the elements of the list:

Index	Name	Description
0	name	User name.
1	passwd	Password info.
2	uid	Id of this user.
3	gid	Group id of this user.
4	quota	Quota information.
5	comment	Comments.
6	gecos	Full name.
7	dir	Home directory.
8	shell	Login shell.
9	expire	Password expiration info.

endpwent

> Ends lookup processing.

getpwent

> Gets next user information.
>
> In scalar context, returns the username.

getpwnam *name*

> Gets information by name.
>
> In scalar context, returns the user id.

getpwuid *uid*

> Gets information by user id.
>
> In scalar context, returns the username.

setpwent Resets lookup processing.

Information About Groups

In list context, each of these routines returns a list of values.
Use the standard module User::grent for by-name access
to the elements of the list:

Index	Name	Description
0	name	Group name.
1	passwd	Password info.
2	gid	Id of this group.
3	members	Space-separated list of the login names of the group members.

endgrent Ends lookup processing.

getgrent Gets next group information.

> In scalar context, returns the group name.

getgrgid *gid*

> Gets information by group id.
>
> In scalar context, returns the group name.

getgrnam *name*

> Gets information by name.
>
> In scalar context, returns the group id.

setgrent Resets lookup processing.

Information About Networks

In list context, each of these routines returns a list of values. Use the standard module Net::netent for by-name access to the elements of the list:

Index	Name	Description
0	name	Network name.
1	aliases	Alias names.
2	addrtype	Address type.
3	net	Network address.

endnetent

> Ends lookup processing.

getnetbyaddr *addr*, *type*

> Gets information by address and type.
>
> In scalar context, returns the network name.

getnetbyname *name*

> Gets information by network name.
>
> In scalar context, returns the network number.

getnetent

> Gets next network information.
>
> In scalar context, returns the network name.

setnetent *stayopen*

> Resets lookup processing.

Information About Network Hosts

In list context, each of these routines returns a list of values. Use the standard module Net::hostent for by-name access to the elements of the list:

Index	Name	Description
0	name	Host name.
1	aliases	Alias names.
2	addrtype	Address type.
3	length	Length of address.
4	addr	Address, or addresses.

endhostent

> Ends lookup processing.

gethostbyaddr *addr , addrtype*

> Gets information by IP address.
>
> In scalar context, returns the hostname.

gethostbyname *name*

> Gets information by hostname.
>
> In scalar context, returns the host address.

gethostent

> Gets next host information.
>
> In scalar context, returns the hostname.

sethostent *stayopen*

> Resets lookup processing.

Information About Network Services

In list context, each of these routines returns a list of values.
Use the standard module Net::servent for by-name access
to the elements of the list:

Index	Name	Description
0	name	Service name.
1	aliases	Alias names.
2	port	Port number.
3	proto	Protocol number.

endservent

> Ends lookup processing.

getservbyname *name , protocol*

> Gets information by service name for the given
> protocol.
>
> In scalar context, returns the service (port) number.

getservbyport *port , protocol*

> Gets information by service port for the given
> protocol.
>
> In scalar context, returns the service name.

getservent
> Gets next service information.
> In scalar context, returns the service name.

setservent *stayopen*
> Resets lookup processing.

Information About Network Protocols

In list context, each of these routines returns a list of values.
Use the standard module Net::protoent for by-name access
to the elements of the list:

Index	Name	Description
0	name	Protocol name.
1	aliases	Alias names.
2	proto	Protocol number.

endprotoent
> Ends lookup processing.

getprotobyname *name*
> Gets information by protocol name.
> In scalar context, returns the protocol number.

getprotobynumber *number*
> Gets information by protocol number.
> In scalar context, returns the name of the protocol.

getprotoent
> Gets next protocol information.
> In scalar context, returns the name of the protocol.

setprotoent *stayopen*
> Resets lookup processing.

Special Variables

The alternative names for special variables are provided by
the standard module English.

The following variables are global and should be localized in subroutines:

$_   Alternative: $ARG.
    The default input, output, and pattern-searching
    space.

$.   Alternatives: $INPUT_LINE_NUMBER, $NR.
    The current input line number of the last filehandle
    that was read from. Reset only when the filehandle
    is closed explicitly.

$/   Alternatives: $INPUT_RECORD_SEPARATOR, $RS.
    The string that separates input records. Default
    value is a newline.

$,   Alternatives: $OUTPUT_FIELD_SEPARATOR, $OFS.
    The output field separator for the print functions.
    Default value is an empty string.

$"   Alternative: $LIST_SEPARATOR.
    The separator that joins elements of arrays
    interpolated in strings. Default value is a space.

$\   Alternatives: $OUTPUT_RECORD_SEPARATOR, $ORS.
    The output record separator for the print functions.
    Default value is an empty string.

$#   The output format for printed numbers. Deprecated.
    Use **printf** instead.

$*   Set to 1 to do multiline matching within strings.
    Deprecated; see the m and s modifiers on page 36.

$?   Alternative: $CHILD_ERROR.
    The status returned by the last ` ... ` command,
    pipe **close**, **wait**, **waitpid**, or **system** function.

$]   The Perl version number, e.g., 5.006. See also $^V
    on page 64.

$[The index of the first element in an array or list, and
    of the first character in a substring. Default is zero.
    Deprecated. Do not use.

$;   Alternatives: $SUBSCRIPT_SEPARATOR, $SUBSEP.
    The subscript separator for multidimensional hash
    emulation. Default is "\034".

$!	Alternatives: $OS_ERROR, $ERRNO. If used in numeric context, yields the current value of errno. Otherwise, yields the corresponding error string.
$@	Alternative: $EVAL_ERROR. The Perl error message from the last **eval** or **do** *expr* command.
$:	Alternative: $FORMAT_LINE_BREAK_CHARACTERS. The set of characters after which a string may be broken to fill continuation fields (starting with ^) in a format.
$0	Alternative: $PROGRAM_NAME. The name of the file containing the Perl script being executed. May be assigned to.
$$	Alternatives: $PROCESS_ID, $PID. The process id of the Perl interpreter running this script. Altered (in the child process) by **fork**.
$<	Alternatives: $REAL_USER_ID, $UID. The real user id of this process.
$>	Alternatives: $EFFECTIVE_USER_ID, $EUID. The effective user id of this process.
$(	Alternatives: $REAL_GROUP_ID, $GID. The real group id of this process.
$)	Alternatives: $EFFECTIVE_GROUP_ID, $EGID. The effective group id, or a space-separated list of group ids, of this process.
$^A	Alternative: $ACCUMULATOR. The accumulator for **formline** and **write** operations.
$^C	Alternative: $COMPILING. True if Perl is run in compile-only mode using command-line option −c.
$^D	Alternative: $DEBUGGING. The debug flags as passed to Perl using command-line option −D.
$^E	Alternative: $EXTENDED_OS_ERROR. Operating system dependent error information.

$^F	Alternative: $SYSTEM_FD_MAX.
	The highest system file descriptor, ordinarily 2.
$^H	The current state of syntax checks.
$^I	Alternative: $INPLACE_EDIT.
	In-place edit extension as passed to Perl using command-line option -i.
$^L	Alternative: $FORMAT_FORMFEED.
	Formfeed character used in formats.
$^M	Emergency memory pool.
$^O	Alternative: $OSNAME.
	Operating system name.
$^P	Alternative: $PERLDB.
	Internal debugging flag.
$^S	Current state of the Perl interpreter.
$^T	Alternative: $BASETIME.
	The time (as delivered by **time**) when the program started. This value is used by the file test operators -M, -A, and -C.
$^V	Alternative: $PERL_VERSION.
	The Perl version as a v-string, e.g., 5.6.0. Use "%vd" format to print it.
$^W	Alternative: $WARNING.
	The value of the -w option as passed to Perl.
$^X	Alternative: $EXECUTABLE_NAME.
	The name by which Perl was invoked.

The following variables are context dependent and need not be localized:

$%	Alternative: $FORMAT_PAGE_NUMBER.
	The current page number of the currently selected output handle.
$=	Alternative: $FORMAT_LINES_PER_PAGE.
	The page length of the current output handle. Default is 60 lines.

$-	Alternative: $FORMAT_LINES_LEFT.

$-   Alternative: $FORMAT_LINES_LEFT.
       The number of lines remaining on the page.

$~   Alternative: $FORMAT_NAME.
       The name of the current report format.

$^   Alternative: $FORMAT_TOP_NAME.
       The name of the current top-of-page format.

$| Alternative: $OUTPUT_AUTOFLUSH.
       If set to nonzero, forces a flush after every write
       or print on the currently selected output handle.
       Default is zero.

$ARGV The name of the current file when reading from <>.

The following variables are always local to the current block:

$&   Alternative: $MATCH.
       The string matched by the last successful pattern
       match.

$`   Alternative: $PREMATCH.
       The string preceding what was matched by the last
       successful match.

$'   Alternative: $POSTMATCH.
       The string following what was matched by the last
       successful match.

$+   Alternative: $LAST_PAREN_MATCH.
       The last bracket matched by the last search pattern.

$1 ... $9 ...
       Contain the subpatterns from the corresponding
       sets of parentheses in the last pattern successfully
       matched. $10 and up are only available if the match
       contained that many subpatterns.

$^R   Alternative: $LAST_REGEXP_CODE_RESULT.
       Result of last (?{ *code* }).

i perldoc perlvar

Special Arrays

The alternative names are provided by the standard module English.

@ARGV   Contains the command-line arguments for the script (not including the command name, which is in $0).

@EXPORT

    Names the methods and other symbols a package exports by default. Used by the Exporter module.

@EXPORT_OK

    Names the methods and other symbols a package can export upon explicit request. Used by the Exporter module.

@F   When command-line option −a is used, contains the split of the input lines.

@INC   Contains the list of places to look for Perl scripts to be evaluated by the do *filename*, **use** and **require** commands.

    Do not modify @INC directly, but use the use lib pragma or −I command-line option instead.

@ISA   List of base classes of a package.

@_   Alternative: @ARG.

    Parameter array for subroutines. Also used by **split** if not in list context.

@−   Alternative: @LAST_MATCH_START.

    After a successful pattern match, contains the offsets of the beginnings of the successful submatches. $−[0] is the offset of the entire match.

@+   Alternative: @LAST_MATCH_END.

    Like @−, but the offsets point to the ends of the submatches. $+[0] is the offset of the end of the entire match.

𝑖 perldoc perlvar

Special Hashes

%ENV   Contains the current environment. The key is the
            name of an environment variable; the value is its
            current setting.

%EXPORT_TAGS
            Defines names for sets of symbols. Used by the
            Exporter module.

%INC   The list of files that have been included with **use**,
            require or **do**. The key is the filename as specified
            with the command; the value is the location of the
            file.

%SIG   Registers signal handlers for various signals. The key
            is the name of the signal (without the SIG prefix);
            the value a subroutine that is executed when the
            signal occurs.
            __WARN__ and __DIE__ are pseudo-signals to attach
            handlers to Perl warnings and exceptions.

%!   Requires the Errno module. Each element of %! has
            a non-zero value only if $! is set to that value.

📖 perldoc perlvar

Environment Variables

Perl uses the following environment variables. This does not
include the environment variables used by library packages.

HOME   Used if **chdir** has no argument.

LC_ALL, LC_CTYPE, LC_COLLATE, LC_NUMERIC,
PERL_BADLANG
            Controls how Perl handles data specific to particular
            natural languages.

LOGDIR   Used if **chdir** has no argument and HOME is not set.

PATH   Used in executing subprocesses, and in finding the
            Perl script if -S is used.

PERL5LIB
            A colon-separated list of directories to look in for

---

Perl library files before looking in the standard library and the current directory.

PERL5DB

The command to get the debugger code.

PERLLIB

Used instead of PERL5LIB if the latter is not defined.

PERL5OPT

Initial (command-line) options for Perl.

PERL5SHELL

The shell that Perl must use internally for executing system commands. Microsoft ports only.

Multithreading

Multithreading requires the standard module Thread. This module implements the join, detach, and yield methods discussed here:

$*thr* -> detach

Detaches a thread so it runs independently.

[$*result* =] $*thr* -> join

Waits for the thread to complete. The value returned is the return value from the thread's subroutine.

lock *variable*

Locks a resource against concurrent access.

$*thr* = new Thread *sub* [*args*]

Creates a new thread that starts executing in the referenced subroutine. The args are passed to this subroutine.

The return value of this subroutine is delivered by the join method.

yield   Explicitly gives up the CPU to some other thread.

Multithreading is an experimental feature. Support for multithreading needs to be built into the Perl executable.

i perldoc perlthrtut

Compiler Backends

To compile a Perl program `foo.pl` with the C backend:

```
perl -MO=C,-ofoo.c foo.pl
```

To compile `foo.pl` with the CC backend:

```
perl -MO=CC,-ofoo.c foo.pl
```

To produce a cross-reference report of the line numbers at which all variables, subroutines, and formats are defined and used:

```
perl -MO=Xref foo.pl
```

To see what Perl compiles your program into:

```
perl -MO=Deparse foo.pl
```

This show exactly the precedence of Perl operators:

```
perl -MO=Deparse,-p foo.pl
```

The compiler backends are experimental.

📖 `perldoc perlcompile`

The Perl Debugger

The Perl symbolic debugger is invoked with `perl -d`.

Any input to the debugger that is not one of the commands enumerated below is evaluated as a Perl expression.

a [*line*] [*command*]
> Sets an action for *line*. Without *command*, clears actions.

A   Deletes all line actions.

b [*line* [*condition*]]
> Sets a breakpoint at *line*; default is the current line.

b *subname* [*condition*]
> Sets a breakpoint at the named subroutine.

b compile *subname*
> Stops after the subroutine is compiled.

b load *file*
> Sets a breakpoint at **require**ing the given file.

b postpone *subname* [*condition*]

    Sets a breakpoint at the first line of the subroutine after it is compiled.

c [*line*] Continues (until *line*, or another breakpoint, or exit).

d [*line*] Deletes the breakpoint at the given line; default is the current line.

D   Deletes all breakpoints.

f *file*   Switches to *file* and starts listing it.

h   Prints out a long help message.

h *cmd* Prints out help for debugger command *cmd*.

h h   Prints out a concise help message.

H [−*number*]

    Displays the last −*number* commands.

l [*range*]

    Lists a range of lines. *range* may be a number, *start−end*, *start+amount*, or a subroutine name. If *range* is omitted, lists the next screenful.

l *subname*

    Lists the named subroutine.

L   Lists lines that have breakpoints or actions.

m *class* Prints the methods callable via the given class.

m *expr*   Evaluates the expression in list context, prints the methods callable on the first element of the result.

man [*topic*]

    View system documentation.

n [*expr*]

    Single steps around the subroutine call.

O [*opt* [= *val*]]

    Sets values of debugger options.

O *opt* ? Queries values of debugger options.

p *expr*† Evaluates *expr* in list context and prints the result. See also x on the facing page.

q	Quits the debugger. An end of file condition on the debugger input will also quit.
r	Returns from the current subroutine.
R	Restarts the debugger.

s [*expr*]

Single steps.

S [!] *pattern*

Lists the names of all subroutines [not] matching the pattern.

t	Toggles trace mode.
t *expr*	Traces through execution of *expr*.
T	Prints a stack trace.

V [*package* [*pattern*]]

Lists variables matching *pattern* in a package. Default package is main.

w [*line*]	Lists a screenful of lines around the specified line.
W	Deletes all watch-expressions.
W *expr*	Adds a global watch-expression.
x *expr*	Evaluates *expr* in list context, dumps the result.

X [*pattern*]

Like V, but assumes the current package.

.	Returns to the executed line.
–	Lists the previous screenful of lines.

= [*alias* [*value*]]

Sets or queries an alias, or lists the current aliases.

/ *pattern* [/]

Searches forward for *pattern*.

? *pattern* [?]

Searches backward for *pattern*.

< *command*

Sets an action to be executed before every debugger prompt. If *command* is ?, lists current actions.

<< *command*

Adds an action to the list of actions to be executed before every debugger prompt.

> *command*

Sets an action to be executed after every debugger prompt. If *command* is ?, lists current actions.

>> *command*

Adds an action to the list of actions to be executed after every debugger prompt.

{ *command*

Defines a debugger command to run before each prompt. If *command* is ?, lists current commands.

{{ *command*

Adds a debugger command to the list of debugger commands to run before each prompt.

! [[-] *number*]

Re-executes a command. Default is the previous command.

! [*pattern*]

Re-executes the last command that started with *pattern*.

!! [*command*]

Runs *command* in a sub-process.

| *cmd*   Runs debugger command *cmd* through the current pager.

|| *cmd*   Same, temporarily **selects** DB::OUT as well.

Pressing the Enter or Return key at the debugger prompt will repeat the last s or n command.

See also PERL5DB on page 68.

The debugger uses environment variables DISPLAY, EMACS, OS2_SHELL, PAGER, SHELL, TERM and WINDOWID, as well as several (internal) variables all starting with PERLDB_.

ℹ perldoc perldebug

Appendix A: Standard Modules

These modules come standard with Perl. A plethora of other modules can be found on the Comprehensive Perl Archive Network, CPAN. See Appendix B, "Perl Links" on page 85 for a list of URLs.

🔢 `perldoc perlmodlib`

> `perldoc` *module* will provide the documentation for the named module.

Platform-independent Modules

`AnyDBM_File`
> Provides a framework for multiple DBM files.

`AutoLoader`
> Load functions only on demand.

`AutoSplit`
> Split a package for autoloading.

`B`
> Experimental package that implements byte compilation, a Perl to C translator, and other interesting things. To be used with the `O` package.

`Benchmark`
> Benchmarks running times of code.

`ByteLoader`
> Loads byte compiler Perl code.

`Carp`   Warns of errors.

`CGI`   Simple Common Gateway Interface Class.

`CGI::Apache`
> Backward compatibility module for `CGI`.

`CGI::Carp`
> Log server errors with helpful context.

`CGI::Cookie`
> Interface to Netscape Cookies.

`CGI::Fast`
> CGI interface for Fast CGI.

`CGI::Pretty`

> Formats the HTML produced by the `CGI` modules.

`CGI::Push`

> Simple interface to Server Push.

`CGI::Switch`

> Simple interface for multiple server types.

`Class::Struct`

> Declares struct-like datatypes as Perl classes.

`Config`   Access to Perl configuration information.

`CPAN`   Maintenance of Perl modules from CPAN sites.

`CPAN::FirstTime`

> Utility for creating the `CPAN` configuration file.

`CPAN::Nox`

> Use with `CPAN`. Runs `CPAN` while avoiding compiled extensions.

`Cwd`   Gets the pathname of the current working directory.

`Data::Dumper`

> Stringifies Perl data structures, suitable for both printing and **eval**.

`DB`   Programmatic interface to the Perl debugging API.

`DB_File`

> Access to Berkeley DB (database) version 1 files.

`Devel::DProf`

> Perl code profiler.

`Devel::Peek`

> A data debugging tool for the XS programmer.

`Devel::SelfStubber`

> Generates stubs for a SelfLoading module.

`Dirhandle`

> Supplies object methods for directory handles.

`Dumpvalue`

> Provides screen dump of Perl data.

`DynaLoader`

> Dynamically loads C libraries into Perl code.

English
: Use verbose English names for punctuation variables.

Env
: Imports environment variables as scalars or arrays.

Errno
: Imports names for system errors.

Exporter
: Implements default import method for modules.

ExtUtils::Command
: Replacements for common Unix commands (for Makefiles).

ExtUtils::Embed
: Utilities for embedding Perl in C/C++ applications.

ExtUtils::Install
: Installs files from here to there.

ExtUtils::Installed
: Inventory management of installed modules.

ExtUtils::Liblist
: Determines libraries to use and how to use them.

ExtUtils::MakeMaker
: Creates an extension Makefile.

ExtUtils::Manifest
: Utilities to write and check a manifest file.

ExtUtils::Miniperl
: Writes the C code for perlmain.c.

ExtUtils::Mkbootstrap
: Makes a bootstrap file for use by DynaLoader.

ExtUtils::Mksymlists
: Writes linker options files for dynamic extension.

ExtUtils::MM_Cygwin
: Methods to override Unix behavior in ExtUtils::MakeMaker.

ExtUtils::MM_OS2
: Methods to override Unix behavior in ExtUtils::MakeMaker.

ExtUtils::MM_Unix
> Methods used by ExtUtils::MakeMaker.

ExtUtils::MM_VMS
> Methods to override Unix behavior in
> ExtUtils::MakeMaker.

ExtUtils::MM_Win32
> Methods to override Unix behavior in
> ExtUtils::MakeMaker.

ExtUtils::Packlist
> Manages packlist files.

ExtUtils::testlib
> Adds blib directories to @INC.

Fatal
> Replaces functions with equivalents that **die** on failure.

Fcntl
> Loads the C fcntl.h defines.

File::Basename
> Parses filenames.

File::CheckTree
> Runs many file checks on a hierarchy of files.

File::Copy
> Copies files or filehandles.

File::DosGlob
> MS-DOS-like globbing (with extensions).

File::Find
> Traverses a hierarchy of files.

File::Glob
> Perl extension for the BSD **glob** routine.

File::Path
> Creates or removes a series of directories.

File::Spec
> Portably performs operations on filenames.

File::Spec::Mac
> Methods for MacOS file specs.

File::Spec::OS2
> Methods for OS/2 file specs.

`File::Spec::Unix`
   Methods used by `File::Spec` for Unix.

`File::Spec::VMS`
   Methods for VMS file specs.

`File::Spec::Win32`
   Methods for Win32 file specs.

`File::stat`
   By name interface to the **stat** functions.

`FileCache`
   Keeps more files open than the system permits.

`FileHandle`
   Supplies object methods for filehandles.

`FindBin` Locates the directory of the Perl script.

`GDBM_File`
   Provides access to the GNU gdbm library.

`Getopt::Long`
   Extended handling of command-line options. Suits all needs.

`Getopt::Std`
   Processes single-character switches with switch clustering.

`IO`   Loads various IO modules.

`IO::Dir`
   Supplies object methods for directory handles.

`IO::File`
   Supplies object methods for filehandles.

`IO::Handle`
   Supplies object methods for I/O handles.

`IO::Pipe`
   Supplies object methods for pipes.

`IO::Seekable`
   Supplies seek-based methods for IO objects.

`IO::Select`
   Object interface to the **select** syscall.

IO::Socket

> Object interface to socket communications.

IPC::Msg

> Interface to System V Message IPC.

IPC::Open2

> Open a pipe to a process for both reading and writing.

IPC::Open3

> Open a pipe to a process for reading, writing, and error handling.

IPC::Semaphore

> Interface to System V semaphores.

IPC::SysV

> System V IPC object class.

JNI::JNI

> Perl encapsulation of the Java Native Interface.

Math::BigFloat

> Arbitrary length float math package.

Math::BigInt

> Arbitrary size integer math package.

Math::Complex

> Complex numbers and associated mathematical functions.

Math::Trig

> Trigonometric functions.

NDBM_File

> **tied** access to NDBM files.

Net::hostent

> Access by name to **gethostent** and friends.

Net::netent

> Access by name to **getnetent** and friends.

Net::Ping

> Checks whether a host is up.

Net::protoent

> Access by name to **getprotoent** and friends.

`Net::servent`
>   Access by name to **getservent** and friends.

`O`   Generic interface to Perl Compiler backends.

`Opcode`   Disables named opcodes when compiling Perl code.

`Pod::Checker`
>   Checks POD documents for syntax errors.

`Pod::Find`
>   Finds POD documents in directory trees.

`Pod::Html`
>   Module to convert POD files to HTML.

`Pod::InputObjects`
>   Objects representing POD input paragraphs, commands, etc.

`Pod::Man`
>   Converts POD data to Unix 'roff' typesetter input.

`Pod::Parser`
>   Base class for creating POD filters and translators.

`Pod::ParseUtils`
>   Helpers for POD parsing and conversion.

`Pod::Plainer`
>   Perl extension for converting POD to old style POD.

`Pod::Select`
>   Extracts selected sections of POD from input.

`Pod::Text`
>   Converts POD data to formatted ASCII text.

`Pod::Text::Color`
>   Converts POD data to formatted color ASCII text.

`Pod::Text::Termcap`
>   Converts POD data to ASCII text with format escapes.

`Pod::Usage`
>   Prints a usage message from embedded POD documentation.

POSIX   Interface to IEEE Std 1003.1, Edition 1(1990).

Safe   Compiles and executes code in restricted compartments.

SDBM_File
        tied access to sdbm files.

Search::Dict
        Searches for key in dictionary file.

SelectSaver
        Saves and restores a selected filehandle.

SelfLoader
        Load functions only on demand.

Shell   Runs shell commands transparently within Perl.

Socket   Loads the C socket.h defines and structure manipulators.

Symbol   Manipulates Perl symbols and their names.

Sys::Hostname
        Tries very hard to get the name of this system.

Sys::Syslog
        Interface to the Unix *syslog* calls.

Term::ANSIColor
        Color screen output using ANSI escape sequences.

Term::Cap
        Perl interface to Unix *termcap*.

Term::Complete
        Word completion module.

Term::ReadLine
        Interface to various readline packages.

Test   Provides a simple framework for writing test scripts.

Test::Harness
        Runs Perl standard test scripts with statistics.

Text::Abbrev
        Creates an abbreviation table from a list.

Text::ParseWords
        Parses text into a list of tokens.

Text::Soundex
> Implementation of the Soundex Algorithm as described by Donald Knuth.

Text::Tabs
> Expands and unexpands tabs.

Text::Wrap
> Line wrapping to form simple paragraphs.

Thread   Implementation of Perl threads.

Thread::Queue
> Implementation of thread-safe queues.

Thread::Semaphore
> Implementation of thread-safe semaphores.

Thread::Signal
> Implementation of reliable signals using threads.

Thread::Specific
> Thread-specific keys.

Tie::Array
> Base class definitions for tied arrays.

Tie::Handle
> Base class definitions for tied filehandles.

Tie::Hash
> Base class definitions for tied hashes.

Tie::RefHash
> Base class for tied hashes with references as keys.

Tie::Scalar
> Base class definitions for tied scalars.

Tie::SubstrHash
> Fixed table-size, fixed key-length hashing.

Time::gmtime
> Access by name to gmtime.

Time::Local
> Efficiently computes time from local and GMT time.

Time::localtime
> Access by name to localtime.

`Time::tm`

>   Internal object for `Time::gmtime` and
>   `Time::localtime`.

`UNIVERSAL`

>   Base class for *all* classes.

`User::grent`

>   Access by name to **getgrent** and friends.

`User::pwent`

>   Access by name to **getpwent** and friends.

Modules For OS/2

`OS2::DLL`

>   Access to DLLs with REXX calling convention and
>   REXX runtime.

`OS2::ExtAttr`

>   Access to extended attributes.

`OS2::PrfDB`

>   Access to the OS/2 settings database.

`OS2::Process`

>   Constants for *system* call on OS/2.

`OS2::REXX`

>   Access to DLLs with REXX calling convention and
>   REXX runtime.

Modules For VMS

`VMS::DCLsym`

>   Perl extension to manipulate DCL symbols.

`VMS::Filespec`

>   Converts VMS and Unix file specifications.

`VMS::Stdio`

>   Standard I/O functions via VMS extensions.

`VMS::XSSymSet`

>   Keeps sets of symbol names palatable to the VMS
>   linker.

Modules For Microsoft Windows

The following modules come standard with ActivePerl, the
Activestate distribution of Perl for Microsoft Windows. These
modules are also available on CPAN.

Win32::ChangeNotify

> Monitors events related to files and directories.

Win32::Console

> Uses Win32 Console and Character Mode Functions.

Win32::Event

> Uses Win32 event objects.

Win32::EventLog

> Processes Win32 Event Logs.

Win32::File

> Manages file attributes.

Win32::FileSecurity

> Manages FileSecurity Discretionary Access Control
> Lists.

Win32::IPC

> Loads base class for Win32 synchronization objects.

Win32::Internet

> Accesses WININET.DLL functions.

Win32::Mutex

> Uses Win32 mutex objects.

Win32::NetAdmin

> Manages network groups and users.

Win32::NetResource

> Manages network resources.

Win32::ODBC

> Uses ODBC Extension for Win32.

Win32::OLE

> Uses OLE Automation extensions.

Win32::OLE::Const

> Extracts constant definitions from TypeLib.

`Win32::OLE::Enum`
> Uses OLE Automation Collection Objects.

`Win32::OLE::NLS`
> Uses OLE National Language Support.

`Win32::OLE::Variant`
> Creates and modifies OLE VARIANT variables.

`Win32::PerfLib`
> Accesses the Windows NT Performance Counter.

`Win32::Process`
> Creates and manipulates processes.

`Win32::Semaphore`
> Uses Win32 semaphore objects.

`Win32::Service`
> Manages system services.

`Win32::Sound`
> Plays with Windows sounds.

`Win32::TieRegistry`
> Mungs the registry.

`Win32API::File`
> Accesses low-level Win32 system API calls for files and directories.

`Win32API::Net`
> Manages Windows NT LanManager accounts.

`Win32API::Registry`
> Accesses low-level Win32 system API calls from `WINREG.H`.

Modules For Other Platforms

For information on modules for other platforms, consult CPAN.

Appendix B: Perl Links

http://www.perl.com/
>   The home of Perl.

http://www.perl.org/
>   Perl advocacy services.

http://www.pm.org/
>   The home of the Perl Mongers, the *de facto* Perl user group.

http://www.cpan.org/
>   Comprehensive Perl Archive Network, CPAN.

http://search.cpan.org/
>   CPAN search engine.

http://news.perl.org/
>   The Perl News site.

http://lists.perl.org/
>   A huge collection of Perl related mailing lists.

http://use.perl.org/
>   A Perl Community news and discussion site.

http://reference.perl.com/
>   A nice collection of Perl resources.

http://bugs.perl.org/
>   The Perl bug database.

http://history.perl.org/
>   Home of CPAST and the Perl Timeline.

http://www.squirrel.nl/perlref.html
>   Home of the *Perl5 Pocket Reference.*

http://www.squirrel.nl/people/jvromans/
>   The author's home.

http://www.itknowledge.com/tpj/
>   The Perl Journal.

http://www.perlmonth.com/
>   Perl Month magazine.

Index